# SAILERS, WHALERS & STEAMERS

A Sunset Book

# SAILERS, WHALERS & STEAMERS

## Ships That Opened the West

by Edith Thacher Hurd

Illustrated by Lyle Galloway

LANE BOOK COMPANY
Menlo Park, California

# ACKNOWLEDGMENTS

The author would like to thank Mr. Karl Kortum, Director of the San Francisco Maritime Museum, without whose advice, guidance, and constant encouragement over a period of several years, this book would never have been written.

The author would also like to thank the staff of the San Francisco Maritime Museum. She is especially grateful to Mr. Albert M. Harmon, Librarian for the Museum; Mrs. Harry Dring; and Miss Theo Jonkel.

The following persons have also been most helpful: Dr. John Barr Tompkins, Head of Public Service, Bancroft Library, Berkeley, California; Mrs. Helen Bretnor, Reference Librarian, Bancroft Library; Miss Dolores Cadell, formerly Head of the Reference Department, San Francisco Public Library; Mr. Harry Dring, Restoration and Maintenance Supervisor, San Francisco Maritime State Historical Monument; and Mr. and Mrs. James H. Frickie, Mill Valley, California.

# INTRODUCTION

The pageant of Pacific Coast seafaring has been slumbering in odd corners of forty volumes and twice that many pamphlets and magazine pieces, clipped and pasted in scrapbooks. No comprehensive book, for man or child, has been written to embrace the story of ships and the West. There are excellent regional maritime histories, and there are substantial books on the subject *being* written, but these are not yet published.

There has been almost no whole knowledge about our shipping out here, and there has been all manner of disproportion and hiatus. Vast categories of square-riggers — the down-Easter and British deepwaterman, for instance — have been overshadowed by clipper ships and have never penetrated the public consciousness. The literally hundreds of two-masted schooners built on the Pacific Coast in the third quarter of the last century are all but unknown, and the three- and four-masters that followed them are only saved from limbo by two of their number that tangibly survive. The builders of these flotillas are forgotten, their achievements strangely obscured. How many people, for instance, realize that a San Francisco Bay shipbuilder, Matthew Turner, launched more vessels than any other shipbuilder in the history of North America?

Edith Hurd has pushed off from shore in an original venture, and although written for children, *Sailers, Whalers, and Steamers* is the first maritime history of the Pacific Coast. It is a success for a number of reasons, but chief among them, in my opinion, is response to a young readership by providing narrative flow. There was need to tell a good story, and the story of our ships, though voluminous, is a good story. Now it has been well and simply told.

If writing a West Coast maritime history *for children* has been a necessity that has been turned into a virtue, the stricture of space has been, too. Writing a comparatively short book has brought the particular into a taut balance with the general. There have had to be omissions, but for the most part, these are of trades, rather than of vessel types. This book, as the title suggests, is about the kind and numbers of our ships. If the ships become real for young readers (and there will be few older readers, too, who can't learn from what Mrs. Hurd and Mr. Galloway have assembled here),then all the rest of the structure that branches forth from an interest in ships — economics, geography, history, literature — will be theirs to pursue.

*Karl Kortum*
DIRECTOR
SAN FRANCISCO MARITIME MUSEUM

# CONTENTS

## CLIPPER SHIPS...GREYHOUNDS OF THE SEA

### The Stag Hound

On a windy morning in May, 1850, the beautiful clipper ship, *Stag Hound,* sailed through the Golden Gate. Her black hull cut through the water. Her huge sails filled with the wind from the sea. Her decks were crowded with eager men, bearded and thin from their passage of almost four months from New York to San Francisco.

Captain Josiah Richardson stood on the afterdeck of the *Stag Hound.* As his ship came to anchor, he looked in amazement at the forest of masts that surrounded him. More than 500 vessels lay rocking at anchor. And a miserable sight they were to the elegant captain of the beautiful clipper ship! Some were old whalers still smelling of whales. Others were old trading ships once used for carrying cowhides from the California coast to the factories of Boston. These were the ships that had brought the farmers, grocers, shoemakers, tailors, butchers, blacksmiths, gamblers, and lawyers around the Horn to California.

8

These ships had brought the men who wanted to be first into the gold fields, the men who didn't care what kind of ship they sailed on, just as long as she was off for "Californy." But many of these would-be miners lived to regret their rush and hurry. The trip around "Cape Stiff," as the sailors called Cape Horn, at the tip of South America, was not a pleasant one. The waves were like mountains. Gales might blow a hundred miles an hour. At times, there were even icebergs to batter the little ships as they fought their way from the Atlantic Ocean into the Pacific Ocean. Many of the ships never made it.

Nevertheless, between December, 1848, and February, 1849, 136 ships sailed from Atlantic ports on the 15,000-mile trip around Cape Horn to San Francisco. Seven hundred and seventy-five vessels, almost all sailing ships, sailed for California in 1849 alone. The average time for these trips was six long months and nineteen days.

When Captain Richardson brought the *Stag Hound* into San Francisco Bay, most of these ships swung idly at anchor. Their crews, and sometimes even their captains, had long since headed for the gold fields. No wonder Captain Richardson looked with surprise and disgust at this ghost fleet, for he commanded one of the fastest, most beautiful ships in the world, built especially for the Gold Rush trade.

## Gold

When James Marshall discovered gold in California in January, 1848, Yerba Buena, the first name the Spaniards gave to San Francisco, was hardly any town at all. About 800 people, Spanish-Californians, Americans, and Indians, lived in wooden shacks and small adobe houses. On the muddy shore of Yerba Buena Cove stood two wharves and a warehouse, which was used for storing furs, cowhides, horns, and tallow, or fat, for making candles. These goods were all the people in Yerba Buena had to trade with the ships from Boston.

For many years, a few Boston ships traded up and down the California coast. On entering a port, a small boat was rowed ashore to bring the rancheros and their wives out to the ship. On the ship were well-stocked shelves and showcases which held many of the things the Californians needed. For sugar, silks, hardware, furniture, combs, shoes, and stockings, the rancheros traded hides, known as California bank notes, and leather bags of tallow.

Sometimes the Boston ships crossed to China for new supplies of silks, tea, spices, and chinaware. Sometimes they sailed to the Sandwich Islands, as Hawaii was then called. Before San Francisco became famous in the Gold Rush, the Sandwich Islands were the center for all trade that was carried on in the Pacific Ocean. American merchants had set up warehouses there and filled them with goods, both from Boston and from China.

When the ships had sold all their goods in the quiet ports of California and filled their holds with hides and tallow, they headed back around the Horn to Massachusetts. It was a slow trade, but a good one, for it supplied the coastal towns with almost everything they needed. But when the Gold Rush hit the little town of Yerba Buena, there wasn't enough of anything for anyone. There wasn't enough food. One egg might cost a dollar. There weren't any clothes to buy. A pair of boots cost about $45. By the time Captain Richardson brought the *Stag Hound* through the Golden Gate, everybody in San Francisco needed something, and they needed it fast!

10

## Smart Men in Boston and New York

Away back East in Boston and New York, shipbuilders and business-men read all about the big excitement out in California. These men knew there was a lot of money to be made if they could cram ships full of boots and shoes, coats and hats, picks and axes, sugar and tea, flour and molasses. If businessmen could fill ships with large enough cargoes and sail them out to California fast enough, they could sell just about anything at any price they pleased.

Smart shipbuilders, such as Donald McKay, William Webb, and Samuel Hall, set to work to build the fastest ships in the world. The ships they began to design and build were called the California Clippers. They were called clippers because they were built to clip through the waves. Because they were long and sleek and slim, they were called greyhounds of the sea. Their bows were sharp and curved in instead of bulging out. Their masts were taller than any that had ever been put in sailing ships. They carried sail after sail of billowing canvas. It was said that a clipper went after the wind instead of waiting for the wind to come to her.

Of the *Witch of the Wave*, on the day she was launched, it was written:

> They say she's bound to sail so fast
> That a man on deck can't catch the mast,
> And a porpoise trying to keep ahead,
> Will get run over and killed stone dead.

The hulls of the clippers were built of wood, sometimes made stronger with bands of iron inside. The hulls were usually painted black, topped with a stripe of gold or crimson. The cabins were finished in white and gold. These ships were streamlined and built with very little decoration, but what they had was beautiful. At the bow of the clipper *Sea Serpent*, a golden eagle spread its wings, and sea serpents were carved across the stern. The *Flying Fish* boasted a fish on the wing at its bow. The *Witchcraft* had a Salem witch on a broomstick. Never before and never since have beautiful ships been given such beautiful names: *Flying Cloud, Eagle Wing, Northern Light,* and *Shooting Star.*

Clipper ship races were the rage of the day. Every ship that left a harbor and every ship that arrived was reported in the newspapers. Money was won and lost betting on the time it would take some clipper to sail from New York or Boston around the Horn to San Francisco. In 1851, the famous *Flying Cloud* made the trip in 89 days and two hours. This record was never beaten, but the *Flying Cloud* made another voyage in exactly the same time, as did the *Andrew Jackson* six years later.

## Not a Coffin

The *Stag Hound* was built in Boston by Donald McKay. She was launched with a bottle of rum on a winter day in December, 1850. Old timers looked at her towering masts and huge sails. They shook their heads in wonder. This was the sharpest clipper ever launched and the biggest merchantman afloat. The shipping world waited to see how she would sail and who would be in command of her. The owners made a wise choice in the quiet-spoken man from Cape Cod, Josiah Richardson. The son of a Harvard College graduate, Captain Richardson had gone to sea as a cabin boy at the age of eleven. By the time he took over the *Stag Hound,* he had spent twenty years as master of schooners, brigs, and other ships. Overnight, he became the most famous shipmaster in the country. When questioned as to how he felt about putting to sea in such a "sharp" ship, the captain replied, "I would not go in the ship at all if I thought she would be my coffin."

Sailing from New York on the first day of February, 1851, Captain Richardson was off the Horn in 49 days and into Valparaiso, Chile, in 66 days. Here he repaired the sails lost in a gale six days out of New York. Despite this delay, the captain was pleased with his beautiful ship, for he wrote to her owners, "The ship has yet to be built that will beat the *Stag Hound.* You have reason to be proud of her, as she is about faultless." With these remarks, Captain Richardson took his ship north to sail through the Golden Gate, 112 days after leaving New York.

After delivering his cargo in San Francisco (which he wrote to his wife he found rather wicked), Captain Richardson set sail for the Orient. The beautiful *Stag Hound* attracted attention wherever she went. In Canton, China, the captain wrote to his wife, "Nearly all the Americans, English, and French have visited the *Stag Hound.* The foreign consuls—English, American—have dined or taken tiffin on board...My cares are not light...I feel most worn down. She [the *Stag Hound*] is now all newly painted, gilt, etc. There is no quiet life here . . . Am thin in flesh."

In Hong Kong, Captain Richardson met up with many old friends, including a Captain Howland who had charge of the *Sea Serpent*. The two ships, being of the new clipper type, caused great excitement as they cleared port within three days of each other, bound for New York. Racing home by way of the Cape of Good Hope, at the tip of Africa, Captain Richardson pounded into New York just ten months and twenty-three days after leaving this port. He was delighted to learn on his arrival that he had beaten the *Sea Serpent*, which did not arrive until six days later. This first voyage paid all the costs of building the *Stag Hound* and put $80,000 besides into the bank account of her owners. No wonder clippers were the rage of the day!

## The Rise and Fall of the Clippers

The great years of the California Clippers were from 1850 to 1860. Thirteen were built in 1852, thirty-one the following year. Captain Richardson commanded one of these, the *Staffordshire*. Taking her whirling around the Horn in 102 days, he carried 120 passengers and a handwritten freight list 13 feet long. In 1853, fifty-one clippers went down the ways of Boston, New York, and other shipyards along the eastern seaboard.

The race to send goods to California began to slow down by 1855. Merchants loaded ships with goods that nobody wanted, or they sent too much of everything. Prices tumbled. Clippers had to wait longer for cargoes and sail farther to find them. By 1860, rumblings of the War between the States filled every newspaper. There was little room for the comings and going of clippers and even less interest in them. The work of the clippers was done. The days of the "greyhounds" were over.

# DOWN-EASTERS

## Bread for Hungry People

Many farmers came to California to get rich by mining gold. They soon found out, however, that there were other ways of making money.

They learned that they could grow the best wheat in the world in the valleys of the Sacramento and the San Joaquin Rivers. They planted wheat, miles and miles of it. The wheat grew, bright green in the spring, tall and golden in the summer.

England, France, Germany, and other countries of Europe wanted California wheat. They wanted wheat as fast as they could get it to make bread for hungry people.

But what kind of ships would be right for carrying grain? Grain was a heavy cargo. It could slide or shift, turning a ship on its side. If grain got wet, it could swell until it burst a ship. Grain sometimes rotted on long voyages, and sometimes it got hot and caught on fire.

## Strong Grain Ships

It had been the shipbuilders of New York and Boston who built the California Clippers, but it was the men of Maine who, in the 1870's, built the strong grain ships. Three thousand miles away from the California grain fields, shipbuilders in Bath and Thomaston built a new kind of ship to carry California grain around the world. Because the new ships were made "way down East" in Maine, they were called down-Easters.

Down-Easters had three masts and were square-rigged. The ribs of the down-Easters were built of white oak from Virginia, and their planking and masts were made of pine from Maine. Although their lines were not so sharp, down-Easters looked like California Clippers.

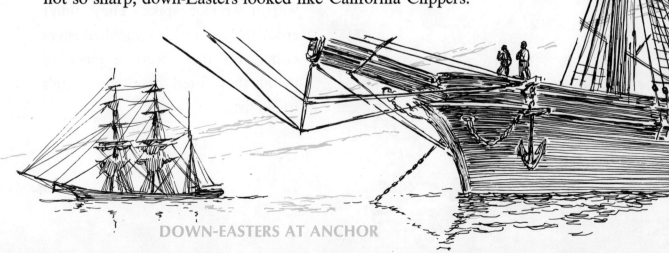

DOWN-EASTERS AT ANCHOR

## The Finest Ships Afloat

From 1870 to 1890, down-Easters were the finest ships afloat. Famous for cleanliness, their rigging and spars were kept in apple-pie order by hard-working crews. As well as being strong enough to carry heavy loads of grain, down-Easters were fast sailers, too. Often they made the trip from California around the Horn to England in less than four months. Earlier vessels had taken an average of six months to make this trip.

Almost all down-Easter captains came from Maine. One small town alone boasted 100 deepwater captains. Sometimes, shipmasters took their wives and children with them and did all they could to make the trips agreeable. Captain Dave Rivers, of the *A. G. Ropes,* allowed his little girl to bring along her pony.

The crew of a down-Easter was usually a mixed lot—a few Americans, plus Swedes, Danes, Irish, and Italians. The mate was called a bucko mate because he had to be able to "lick his weight in wildcats." The crew didn't care to taste his belaying pin soup, a crack on the head with a wooden spike. They didn't enjoy the feel of his knuckle-dusters either, for these were a piece of metal that fitted over the mate's tough fist.

By 1890, San Francisco was the third most important sailing port in all the world. At certain times of the year, as many as 100 down-Easters might be loading grain in San Francisco harbor within a few months of one another. Only Liverpool, in England, and the coal port of Newcastle, in Australia, saw more ships come and go.

## Ice for India

Not only did the down-Easters carry grain, but they also sailed fertilizer from South America to European farmers. Sometimes they filled their holds with ice, packed in tons and tons of sawdust, and sailed it from Maine to India. A number of the big square-riggers sailed to China and Japan with tins of kerosene for lanterns. This was called the case oil trade because of the wooden box, or case, the cans were packed in. One smart down-Easter captain had a locomotive hoisted on his deck and carried it out to Hong Kong.

Down-Easters sailed home again with rice from India, silks and tea from China, and hemp (for making rope) from Manila. Coal and tallow were brought back from Australia. Many down-Easters went into the Hawaiian sugar trade, bringing tons of sugar from the Islands to the United States. Old logs, diaries, and letters tell of the entertainments, dinners, dances, and gay parties held by visiting Maine captains in the far ports of the world—Shanghai, Hong Kong, and Bombay.

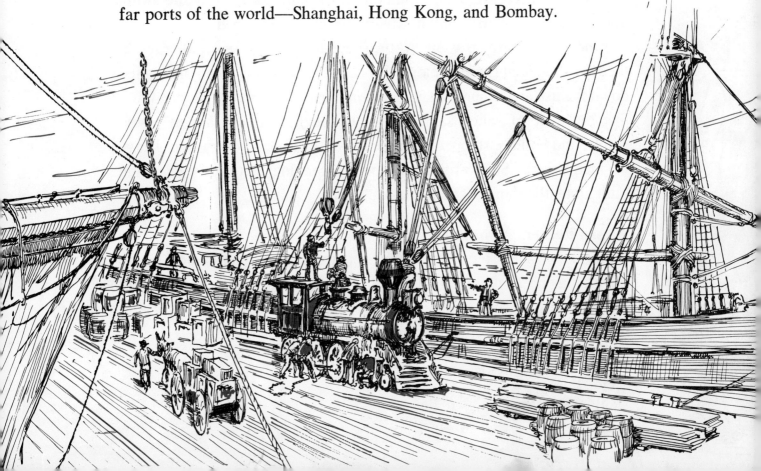

### England Takes Away the Trade

The men of Maine were proud of their down-Easters, for they had carried tons and tons of grain to make bread for hungry people. Nevertheless, the great days of the down-Easters began to draw to a close when English and Scotch shipyards built iron ships, nicknamed by sailors, lime juicers, and sent them west to carry California grain. Down-Easters then had to find other work to do. Some went into the lumber trade and carried Douglas fir from Washington and Oregon to Australia. A few joined the Alaska Packers' fleet to work as supply ships for the Alaska salmon canneries.

By 1900, most of the down-Easters claimed a Western city as home port. Instead of Boston, New York, or a seaport town in Maine, the down-Easters carried the name of a Pacific port, such as San Francisco, Portland, Seattle, or Tacoma lettered on their sterns. But not one of this great fleet of beautiful square-riggers built in Maine is left today.

# STARS OF THE SEA

### Friday Fish

In 1867, the United States bought Alaska from the Russians for $7,200,000. There were more salmon off the coast of Alaska and swiming up Alaskan rivers than anywhere else in all the world.

American fishermen went north to set nets in the sea and traps in the rivers to catch these salmon. The early fishermen cleaned and salted down the fish and brought them home in barrels. But many people didn't like the taste of salted salmon. They thought canned salmon tasted better, and besides, shippers found cans were easier to carry than heavy wooden barrels. So it wasn't long before canning factories were being built along the shores of cold Alaska.

### Alaska Packers Association

The Alaska Packers Association set up many canneries and began buying strong ships to sail the 2,000 miles of stormy seas from San Francisco to Alaska. At first they bought fine old down-Easters. Later they bought strong iron lime juicers.

The Alaska Packers' fleet was called the "Star" fleet: *Star of England, Star of India, Star of Alaska,* and many more. In all, there were nineteen *Stars* in the famous fleet.

In winter, the fleet tied up in the Oakland Creek, now called the Oakland Estuary, across the bay from San Francisco. It headed north each spring. The ships went heavy-laden, for they wouldn't return until September or October. Sometimes as many as 300 workers were jam-packed together on one ship: Italians and Scandinavians to do the fishing; Germans to take care of the canning machinery; Chinese and Mexicans to clean and can the fish.

Although the big salmon ships were at sea only about two months out of every year, these months could be full of dangers. Many ships were caught in the ice. Some were wrecked on the rocky shores.

Finally, steam-driven ships took over the work of the old down-Easters and the iron and steel salmon packets. Today, men are flown in airplanes to Alaska to fish and do the canning in the spring. There are only two *Stars* left now. The *Star of Alaska,* her name changed back to the original, *Balclutha,* has been bought and restored by the San Francisco Maritime Museum and can be seen at Fisherman's Wharf in San Francisco. The *Star of India* belongs to the Maritime Museum Association of San Diego and is on exhibit there.

*Normally two men handled the Columbia River salmon boats, which were called gill-netters because the salmon were caught by their gills in the nets. The fishermen cooked on a little stove in their boat and made their sails into a tent.*

# LIME JUICERS

### Steel Ships

Lime juicers were great iron and, later, steel ships built in England and Scotland. Many of them were built for the California grain trade. The name "lime juicer" came from the custom, not found on American ships, of giving the crew a pannikin, or cup, of lime juice and water every day. This kept the men from getting scurvy, a terrible disease due to lack of fresh fruits and vegetables. Scurvy causes the gums to rot and the teeth to drop out. It makes a man's body stiffen up in dreadful pain.

The hulls of the lime juicers were built of iron and steel plates, less than one inch thick. These metal hulls left more room for cargo than did the thick wooden hulls of the down-Easters. Steel ships were also less expensive to keep up. Worms couldn't eat the hulls. They leaked less. Fire could burn only their wooden decks.

It is not surprising that the new lime juicers began to take the grain trade away from the down-Easters. Between 1881 and 1885, only 418 wooden American ships loaded grain in San Francisco; whereas, 761 British ships, almost all of them built of iron and steel, loaded grain there. Among these ships were the two great lime juicers, the *Falls of Clyde,* which is on view today in Honolulu, Hawaii, and the *Balclutha.*

## The Balclutha

The *Balclutha* was a typical lime juicer, or British deepwaterman. She was built in Glasgow, Scotland, in 1886, to carry California grain. This strong iron ship made seventeen trips around the Horn and wandered other parts of the world for many years. She carried Douglas fir from Puget Sound to Australia for a northern lumber company. She returned with her hold full of coal for the Pacific coastwise steamers and the locomotives of the Southern Pacific Railroad.

On a cold and misty night in May, 1903, the *Balclutha* struck a hidden reef near Kodiak Island, off the coast of Alaska. The crew was saved, but the *Balclutha* had to be abandoned. The Alaska Packers Association bought her where she lay for $500. They patched her up and sailed her down to San Francisco where they repaired her damaged hull and renamed her the *Star of Alaska*. For many years, the *Star of Alaska* was the fastest *Star* in the fleet.

## Brassbounders and Ship's Boys

On a British ship like the *Balclutha,* the young "brassbounders" lived in the afterend of the deckhouse. Brassbounders were British boys of 15 to 20 who were learning the trade of the sea. Often terribly homesick and seasick, these young apprentice officers were seldom shown favor. They were expected to do men's work and to step lively, no matter how they might feel inside. "One hand for yourself, and one for the ship. Keep your eye on your job, and don't look down." This was the wise advice of an old seaman to a young brassbounder going aloft for the first time, for the boys were sent to the top of the mainmast to loosen the main royal as soon as the ship put to sea. The main royal was usually the smallest sail on the ship, but it hung 130 feet above the deck. With only this sail to loosen and furl, the boys were supposed to get used to the roll of the ship, to moving on the yards, and to climbing in the rigging.

Although the captains were to teach the boys navigation, not all the captains were the teacher type! The brassbounders often had to learn what they could for themselves. On American ships, these young apprentices were known as ship's boys. They lived aft with the captain and mates. If the ship's boys were willing to learn and work hard, they could rise to the rank of second mate, mate, and sometimes to captain.

But the boys' lives were not all hardship when they once got used to the ship. There were the sing-songs during the dogwatch (early evening). There were the sea yarns told by the sailors. There was the excitement of faraway ports where notorious innkeepers often shanghaied, or kidnapped, sailors to fill the crew of a sailing vessel. These innkeepers collected the innocent sailors' future wages as blood money. The boys of the British ship *Springburn* took revenge on a famous crimp of San Francisco named "Shanghai Brown." They kidnapped him and sent him around the Horn in midwinter. A favorite chanty tells of this adventure:

Who do you think is the master of her?
Blow, boys, blow!
Shanghai Brown, the sailor robber.
Blow, my bully boys, blow!

*Wheel for steering the ship: As many as four men might be required to handle the wheel in a bad storm.*

③

②

*Charthouse: a small deck-house in which the captain kept all the charts for plotting the ship's course. In heavy weather, the captain often remained here for days without going below to sleep.*

*A Typical Limejuicer Similar to the Balclutha and Star of India*

*Captain's cabin, dining saloon, and bathroom: These quarters were often very elegant with walls paneled in fine woods, a carpet on the floor, and a regular bedstead. Many captains brought their wives to sea. A baby girl was even born aboard the Balclutha.*

**4**

Forecastle ("fo'c'sle"): 15 or 20 seamen lived here. It served as their parlor, dining room, and bedroom where they kept all they owned in their big sea chests. The sailors shared this small place with the windlass, which was used to hoist the anchor.

Deckhouse: a small, covered house on deck where the sailmaker, the carpenter, and the cook lived. All food was prepared in the galley on a big iron stove.

**5**

**5**

**4**

**6**

**6**

The men are walking around the capstan to hoist anchor.

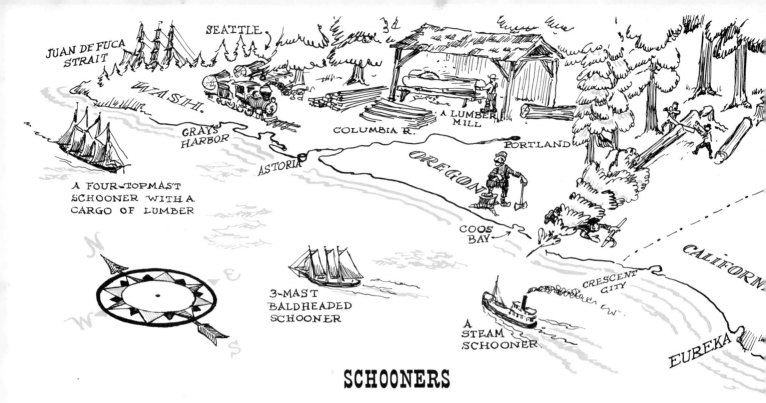

A FOUR-TOPMAST SCHOONER WITH A CARGO OF LUMBER

3-MAST BALDHEADED SCHOONER

A STEAM SCHOONER

JUAN DE FUCA STRAIT

SEATTLE

WASH.

GRAYS HARBOR

COLUMBIA R.

A LUMBER MILL

PORTLAND

ASTORIA

OREGON

COOS BAY

CRESCENT CITY

CALIFORNIA

EUREKA

# SCHOONERS

### Adobe Won't Do

Houses, houses, houses. Everybody needs a house to live in. Everybody needs a house to eat in and to keep warm and dry in. The early Spanish settlers in California built their houses out of clay bricks. These made nice adobe houses, cool houses with courtyards and gardens. These were houses for slow, quiet, easy living. This was the way the Spaniards liked to live in California.

Then came the rough and restless young Americans. They came by ship. They came by trail across the plains. These men did not want to lead a slow and easy life. They couldn't wait for clay to dry.

Lumber, lumber, lumber. Everybody needed lumber to build the booming town of San Francisco and the booming little towns growing up around the mines. Stores, hotels, restaurants, and dance halls—that's what they needed lumber for. Lumber came around the Horn on ships, but that was mighty slow. Trees were chopped along the shores of San Francisco Bay, but not enough.

Trappers, miners, hunters began exploring up and down the coast of California, Oregon, and Washington. "There's trees enough up there to build a thousand towns." That was what they said about the great stands of redwood trees, north of San Francisco in Sonoma and along the Mendocino Coast, and the huge Douglas firs in Oregon and Washington.

26

THREE-MASTED BALDHEADED SCHOONER (NO TOPMASTS)

OVER 125 THREE-MASTERS WERE BUILT ON THE PACIFIC COAST

the Dog Holes and Lumber Ports of the North Pacific Coast

ONE-TOPMAST SCHOONER LOADING LUMBER BY CHUTE

OXEN HAULING LOGS FROM THE FOREST

SACRAMENTO R.

SAN PABLO BAY

SAN FRANCISCO BAY

SCOW SCHOONER

SAN FRANCISCO

FT. BRAGG

MENDOCINO

NOYO

ALBION

GREENWOOD

Pt. Arena

GUALALA

FT. ROSS

Bodega Hd.

Pt. Reyes

Drakes Bay

4-MAST BARKENTINE A FAVORITE OF PACIFIC COAST SAILORS

4-MAST BARK-RIGGED LIMEJUICER

It wasn't easy work, this lumbering. Redwood trees and Douglas firs were very, very tall. Fifty men standing on one another's shoulders could just reach the top branch of an average redwood. Four men holding hands *might* reach around the trunk. These trees were cut with handsaws and axes. There were no chain saws in those days. If the trees grew near a river, they were floated to the mills when the spring rains came. If they grew too far from water, long, slow teams of ten or twelve oxen dragged the logs out of the forests on skid roads made of logs and grease and mud.

Lime juicers and down-Easters sailed into Puget Sound and up the Columbia River to take out Douglas fir. But the lime juicers and down-Easters were too large to go near the rocky coast of northern California. It took a smaller ship to do this job.

FOUR-TOPMAST SCHOONER WITH RINGTAIL SET ON JIGGER TOPMAST

OVER 180 FOUR-MASTERS WERE BUILT ON THE PACIFIC COAST

## Two-Masted Schooners

The vessels that were built to sail close to the rocky coast of California where the redwood forests grew were two-masted schooners. These tiny ships were often called the work horses of the Pacific. They were fore-and-aft-rigged instead of square-rigged. This made them easier to handle when they entered the small openings of the coast to pick up redwood lumber. It also took a smaller crew to man a schooner than it did to man a big lime juicer or down-Easter.

More than five hundred two-masted schooners were built by San Francisco shipbuilders and the shipbuilders of the north Pacific Coast. The shipbuilders called these little schooners outside porters because they sailed into outside ports, or dog holes.

### Dog Holes and Bar Ports

"Dog hole" was a nickname given to tiny openings, or nooks, in the rocky cliffs along the northern California coast. "There's hardly room enough for a dog to turn around in one of those," the sailors said. Dog holes dotted the Sonoma and Mendocino Coast, from San Francisco, north to Humboldt Bay.

Loading lumber in a dog hole was dangerous work. There was seldom a pier for a vessel to tie up to. Wind and waves would have smashed a pier to pieces. For this reason, chutes, or slides, were built from the high rocky cliffs to where the ships anchored below. The lumber was then slid, board by board, down the chute to the schooners.

Later, more and more schooners loaded lumber by using long wires stretched from a tower ashore to an anchor on the opposite side of the dog hole. Lumber was let down the wire to the schooner. This was known as loading under the wire.

29

Captains had to enter the dog holes with great care. Heavy fogs, strong winds, and dangerous currents swept the coast. Once inside the dog hole, a captain had to watch the weather, for he could not allow his ship to be caught in a dog hole when a storm was blowing up. It was safer to chop the anchor rope, hoist the sails, and be off to the open sea than to risk being smashed to kindling wood on the rocky shore.

A bar port was a harbor with a long and dangerous strip of sand that ran across its entrance. These sand bars were dangerous, not only because of the shallow water which covered them, but because of the great waves that often broke over them. The steam schooner, *San Gabriel,* waited almost two months before she was able to cross the Umpqua River bar. Humboldt Bay, Coos Bay, the Columbia River, and Grays Harbor were the most important bar ports on the West Coast.

It took brave captains and good crews to sail in and out of the dog holes and the bar ports. But the schooners were a welcome sight to the men and women in the small lumber towns because they were often the only link the people had with San Francisco.

*The harbor that nature had provided Los Angeles at San Pedro was too small for the growing city. To make the harbor larger, many years were spent building a 12-mile curving breakwater out into the ocean. The C. A. Thayer is shown arriving in San Pedro as rocks the size of automobiles are being dumped to make this largest man-made harbor in the world. (The C. A. Thayer has been restored by the San Francisco Maritime Museum Association and the State Division of Beaches and Parks. She can be seen at the Hyde Street Pier in San Francisco.)*

## Larger Schooners for Longer Hauls

The small two-masted schooners were just right for carrying redwood lumber from the dog holes and closer bar ports on the short trip to San Francisco. Then, as the builders of California learned more about the wonderful Douglas fir of Oregon and Washington, bigger schooners were needed to make the long voyage from the northern forests to southern California. Larger two-masted, and, later, three-masted schooners were built to sail Douglas fir to the fast growing towns of Santa Barbara, San Pedro (which was the port for Los Angeles), and San Diego.

Five three-masted schooners were built in 1875, and many more were launched during the next thirty years. Among these, the *Wawona,* which was built by Hans Bendixsen, is now on view in Seattle, Washington. Hans Bendixsen also built a sister ship to the *Wawona,* named the *C. A. Thayer.* The *Thayer* led a busy life carrying lumber from Grays Harbor, in Washington, to ports along the California coast.

Life on a lumber schooner was often a pleasant one. The crew of four to six seamen lived in a small forecastle forward. The captain, and sometimes his wife, lived in a cabin at the stern. This cabin was often both the living quarters and the captain's office. There might be a phonograph to play on long evenings, or perhaps a sweet-singing bird in a cage for the captain's wife to enjoy. A bathroom next to their cabin was reserved for the captain and his wife. They were served hot food brought aft from the galley in a basket. Their comfortable dining saloon was kept warm by a coal stove, known as a Hot Pot.

In time, even three-masted schooners were not large enough to carry all the lumber that was needed in California and in other ports around the world. California shipbuilders turned to making larger schooners, schooners with four or even five masts. They also liked a new type of vessel called a barkentine. Barkentines looked like schooners, but the first mast was square-rigged. This made the ship easier to handle and a little faster than a schooner.

**TWO-MASTED SCHOONER (A ONE-TOPMAST SCHOONER)**

**TOPSAIL SCHOONER RARE ON THE WEST COAST**

**BRIGANTINE MUCH USED IN THE PACIFIC ISLAND TRADE**

**FIVE-MASTED SCHOONER**

**BARKENTINE**

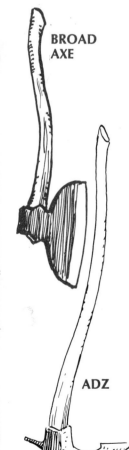

**BROAD
AXE**

**ADZ**

**SLICK**

**HAWSING BEETLE**

### Who Built These Ships?

It was the famous shipbuilders of New York and Massachusetts who built the clipper ships. The men of Maine built the strong down-Easters. But it was the shipbuilders of California, Oregon, and Washington who built the sturdy schooners to carry Pacific Coast lumber.

Most of these West Coast shipbuilders learned their trade either in Europe or the New England states. Hans Bendixsen and Thomas H. Peterson came from Denmark. The Dickie brothers came from Scotland, and the Hall brothers from Massachusetts.

When these men came out to the West Coast, they knew they had to build a different kind of ship than they had ever built before. They knew they had to build a ship with strong decks to carry loads of heavy fir and redwood. They had to build ships that could sail into the dangerous Columbia River and other bar ports. These ships had to be able to stand against the pounding waves of the dog holes in northern California and the outside ports of southern California. Many of these men were fine shipmasters as well as fine shipbuilders. They knew the difference between weather on the Atlantic Coast and weather on the Pacific Coast.

These shipbuilders set up their shipyards where lumber was easy to get and, therefore, would not cost too much. Thomas Peterson built vessels right on the small beaches of the dog holes on the Mendocino Coast. The Dickie brothers built the *Bowhead* and many other vessels at their shipyard on San Francisco Bay. Hans Bendixsen built 150 vessels at Humboldt Bay, where he was close to the best lumber, including Douglas fir. The Hall brothers went north to set up their shipyard near Seattle and turned out more than 100 vessels. Their four-masted schooners were thought by sailing captains to be the finest on the Coast. Matthew Turner, perhaps the best known shipbuilder in the West, started building his ships at a yard in San Francisco. He later moved north to Benicia, where he used the old Pacific Mail Steamship yard. Turner's shipyards turned out 228 vessels. This was more ships than had ever been turned out by any other shipyard in the history of North America.

*The last of the scow schooners, the* Alma, *can be seen today at the Hyde Street Pier in San Francisco where she has been restored by the Maritime Museum and the State Division of Beaches and Parks. Scow schooners had flat bottoms, which made it easier for them to sail in shallow water as they carried hay, bricks, lumber, and grain from cities around San Francisco Bay to San Francisco. The steersman of a scow schooner sometimes stood on a ladder in the stern in order to see over a tall deckload of baled hay.* 33

## Steam Schooners

*Surprise* was the name of the first steam schooner built in California. She was built in 1884, by Charles G. White, at North Beach, San Francisco. It must have been a surprise indeed to many a sailing-ship captain to see these new schooners speed through the water without a sail in sight. A schooner that ran by steam did not have to wait for wind or weather. It could steam north from San Francisco in shorter time than a sailing ship, which had to beat against the northwest wind. This wind blows down and against the coast at least six months out of the year. Steam schooners were also easier to handle in the small harbors of the redwood coast. They could get into port more easily than sailing ships. They could get out more quickly if caught by a sudden storm.

Between 1885 and 1923, 225 wooden steam schooners were built on the West Coast. Especially after the San Francisco earthquake and fire of 1906, large numbers of these vessels were built to carry the lumber that was needed to rebuild the city. The only wooden steam schooner left today is the *Wapama*. This schooner can be seen at the Hyde Street Pier in San Francisco, where she has been restored by the Maritime Museum and the State Division of Beaches and Parks.

## WHALERS

## EARLY WHALERS

**A Nantucket Sleigh Ride**

"Blows!" comes the call from the masthead.

"Where away?" answers the captain.

"Three points off the lee bow."

Four small boats go over the side. The men jump to their places. The mate takes up his long steering oar.

Quietly, carefully, one little boat comes close to the spouting whale.

The mate gives an order. A harpoon shoots through the air. Out goes the line. The whale swims, faster, faster, faster. The little whaleboat cuts through the water, off on a "Nantucket sleigh ride."

The whale tires at last. The boat comes close. The mate stands ready in the bow.

One, two, three! He throws his lance mightily.

35

**SPERM WHALE**

Blood covers the water.

The great whale is dead.

The black body is towed back to the ship. The blubber, or fat, is stripped off and boiled down in black kettles on the deck. The whalebone is cut out and stored below.

When the casks are filled with oil, when the hold is heavy with whalebone, the ship returns home. The long voyage is over.

## Whalers Open the Pacific

The earliest American whalers sailed from the island of Nantucket, off the coast of Cape Cod, in Massachusetts. Later, they chose the deeper harbor of the small town of New Bedford on the mainland. New Bedford grew as a whaling center until, by 1847, it boasted 254 whalers.

In the early 1820's, these whalers sailed around the Horn to hunt for sperm whales in Pacific waters. Then on they went to the newly discovered Japan Grounds, as the waters off Japan were called. In the 1830's and 1840's, the whalers pushed northward to look for the bowhead and the mighty right whale. The whalers tracked these whales in the Gulf of Alaska, through the Bering Straits, and into the Bering Sea. When their water casks were almost empty, their food a barrel or two of wormy pilot bread, the whalers made their way back to Honolulu and Lahaina, favorite harbors in Hawaii, or back to California.

## El Puerto de los Balleneros — Sausalito

The little town of Yerba Buena welcomed these whalers, for whale-ships had been anchoring here for twenty-five years before the Gold Rush started. In fact, before 1848, most of the vessels flying the American flag on the coast of California were either trading ships from Boston or whalers from New England. Often more whalers than traders were to be found at Yerba Buena or anchored off the Richardson ranch at Sausalito.

William Richardson had also been a mate on a British whaling ship before he settled down in California and married the beautiful Spanish señorita, Maria Antonia. Whalers were always welcome at the Richardson ranch, where they could refill their water casks from a spring full of water so pure that it was known to whalers all over the Pacific. Old logs and letters tell of the beauties of the Richardson ranch and speak of Sausalito as a "good wood and watering place." A captain wrote to his wife that he had spent $131.50 buying "223 pumpkins, five bullocks, fowls, beans, and corn" for his ship at Sausalito. The Richardson ranch and its well-sheltered cove welcomed so many whaleships that it became known as el puerto de los balleneros, the port of the whalers.

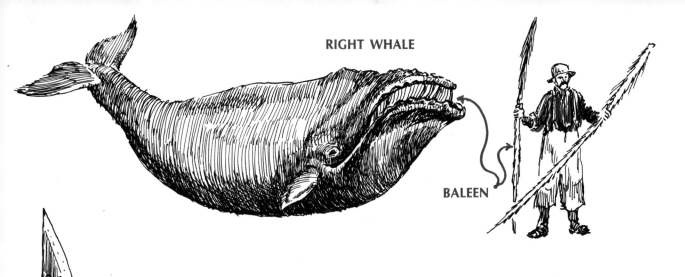

RIGHT WHALE

BALEEN

HARPOONS

## Shore Whaling on the California Coast

There was no whaling at all in the Bay of San Francisco, but there were plenty of humpback whales off the little Spanish capital of Monterey in California. Here was good shore whaling. Sometimes as many as forty little whaleboats rowed or sailed from the harbor at one time.

To the south of Monterey, near San Diego, the gray whale rode the surf close to the shore in order to scratch off the tiny sea animals that clung to its back. The gray whales also came south from the Arctic every summer to give birth to their calves. In the warm water off the coast of southern California, many a whaleboat put out from the beaches of San Diego to chase a gray whale and returned to boil down the blubber in huge iron pots on the shore.

## The Mighty Right Whale and the Bowhead

As the gray whale and the sperm whale of the Pacific grew harder and harder to find, the whalers turned north in search of the mighty right whale and the bowhead. The right whale was the whale that a captain described in a letter to his wife as "mighty whales which swim in a sea of water and have a sea of oil swimming in them." The bowhead was a deadly, angry, ugly whale. His mouth turned down in a snarl. His body was covered with patches of white, which made him look like a piebald horse. His head was full of oil. His mouth was filled with whalebone. The bowhead lived in the Arctic North with icebergs so large they could crush a small ship like a matchstick. He lived in a land of blizzards so fierce that ships could be buried forever beneath them. In 1871, thirty-two whalers were caught and crushed in the ice. Five years later, twelve more ships were lost in the icy land of the bowhead whale.

### The New Bedford of the Pacific

When the railroad crossed the country in 1869, the whalers began to bring their oil to San Francisco. Railroad tank cars could carry the oil back East in half the time and twice as safely as the whaling ships could sail it around the Horn. More and more whalers began to call San Francisco home port. The Oakland Estuary, across the Bay from San Francisco, became the whalers' wintering place. The business offices were moved from New Bedford, Massachusetts, out to San Francisco. Shipyards sprang up to build new ships and to repair the old ones. Between 1880 and 1900, San Francisco was the largest whaling center in the world. It was often called the New Bedford of the Pacific.

## STEAM WHALERS

### Igloos on the Ice

In 1882, the Dickie brothers' shipyard in San Francisco built the first steam whaler on the Pacific Coast. This new vessel was built for the Pacific Steam Whaling Company, who named her the *Bowhead*. Although this was a new type of whaleship in the West, the Dickie brothers came from Scotland, where steam whaling barks had been built for many years.

The *Bowhead* had three masts, an auxiliary steam engine, and a bow made of oak and iron. There was steam heat in the captain's cabin and steam heat to warm the crew in the forecastle. Here was a ship strong enough to stand against the cold, the ice, and the terrible storms of an Arctic winter.

CUTTING
SPADE

LANCE

THE "BOWHEAD"

39

The *Bowhead* sailed from San Francisco for the Arctic Sea on April 12, 1882. She came back in November, having caught seventeen whales in seven months. "The floating tea kettle of the polar sea," as the *Bowhead* was called, had proven that steam-driven vessels were better than pure sailing ships for Arctic whaling.

After the success of the *Bowhead,* several more steam whaling barks were built in San Francisco, each named for a different kind of whale: *Orca, Narwhal,* and *Balaena.* In order to save coal, these vessels used their sails when going north and coming home. But steam was better than sails when a ship was caught in the ice or had to slip between two icebergs. It was easier and safer to break up an ice field with a good steam engine and a bow of oak and iron than with a wooden sailing ship.

The steam whalers could also stay in the Arctic Sea for longer periods of time than sailing ships. Trips to Herschel Island, around the bulge of Alaska on the dreary coast of Canada, often lasted one, or even two years. When the whaleships stopped to winter at Herschel Island, their decks were covered with wooden roofs. Snow piled so deeply on top that the ships looked like huge igloos floating on a sea of ice.

Sometimes twenty ships or more tied up together to wait the long, dark winter through. A few captains brought their wives along. There were parties, dances, cards, concerts, and even coasting on the ice. One captain held a baseball game to celebrate the Fourth of July.

The Eskimos were glad to have a little company. They gathered up their wives and children and built small shacks along the shore. They shot deer, elk, or geese to feed the whalers. Driftwood served as fuel.

It was a cold and rugged life, but one young wife told friends when she came home, "It was a delightful trip. The ship was comfortable, and we had a really splendid crew. Officers and men were kind—the ship was like the home of one big family."

## Oil from the Ground

After 1900, the need for whale oil grew less and less. A new kind of oil, called petroleum, had been discovered in the ground and was being pumped out by the barrelful.

It was easier and cheaper to pump oil from the ground than to go hunting whales in the cold Arctic Sea. Whalebone, which had been used in corsets, canes, and carriage whips, was less in demand. Ladies were not wearing as many corsets as they used to. Men did not carry canes or use carriage whips any more. A new material, called celluloid, was being used to make many of the things that had been made of whalebone.

Fewer whaling ships went north each spring. Many were laid up in the Oakland Creek. Some were sold and rebuilt to carry case oil in World War I, when ships were scarce. The old *Narwhal* was sold to the motion picture industry. The *Charles W. Morgan* was a whaler that had sailed all seas for over sixty years. She spent seventeen of these years going to and from San Francisco. Today she is the only true whaler left and can be seen at the whaling museum in Mystic, Connecticut.

Modern whaling is done from a floating factory, which is almost as long as an aircraft carrier. The whales are killed with harpoons that carry bombs. The harpoons are fired from a cannon mounted in the bow of a small, fast ship known as a killer boat. Nobody yells, "She blows!" Nobody dances through the night on the deck of a ship that looks like an igloo floating in the Arctic ice.

BUGGY
WHIPS

OIL FOR
LAMPS

GRANDMA'S
CORSET

OIL FOR WATCHES

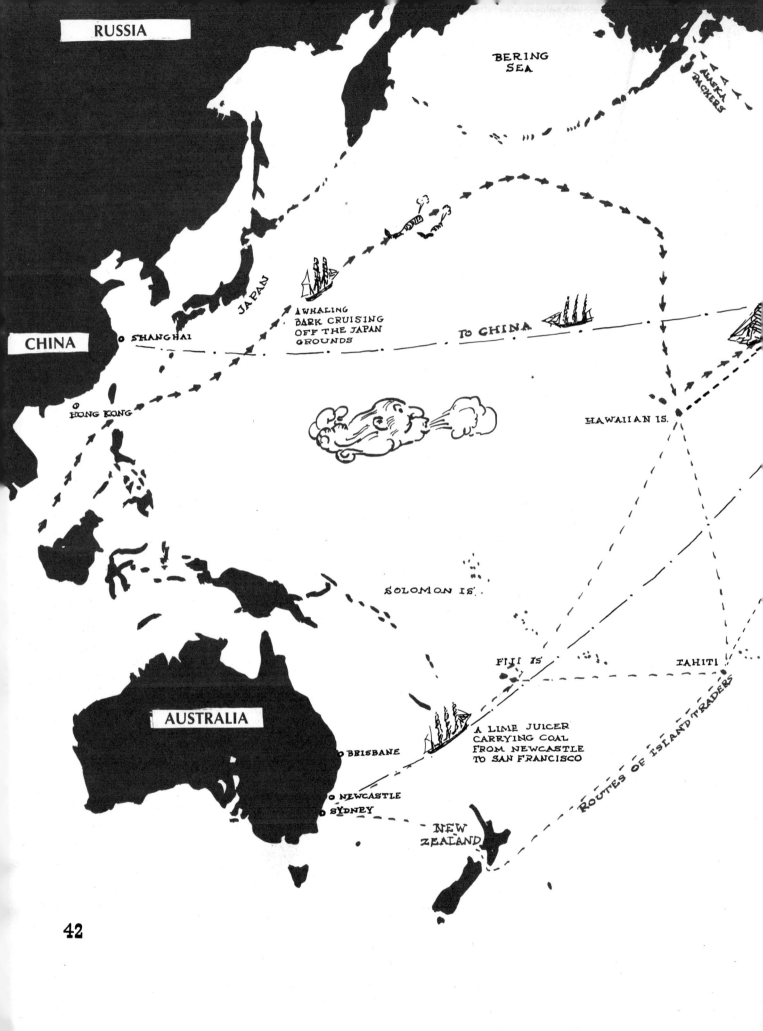

RUSSIA

BERING
SEA

ALASKA PACKERS

JAPAN

CHINA

SHANGHAI

A WHALING
BARK CRUISING
OFF THE JAPAN
GROUNDS

TO CHINA

HONG KONG

HAWAIIAN IS.

SOLOMON IS.

FIJI IS.

TAHITI

AUSTRALIA

BRISBANE

A LIME JUICER
CARRYING COAL
FROM NEWCASTLE
TO SAN FRANCISCO

NEWCASTLE

SYDNEY

NEW
ZEALAND

ROUTES OF ISLAND TRADERS

CANADA

UNITED
STATES

SEATTLE

COASTAL
SHIPPING

SAN
FRANCISCO

LOS
ANGELES

SAN DIEGO

BOSTON

NEW YORK

A BARKENTINE
WITH A CARGO
OF LUMBER FOR
HAWAII

A CLIPPER SHIP
OUT OF NEW YORK
BOUND FOR SAN FRANCISCO

A BRIGANTINE
BOUND FOR
TAHITI

SOUTH
AMERICA

CALLAO

THE
SPERM WHALE
BLOWS

NITRATE
PORTS

ANTOFAGASTA

RIO DE
JANEIRO

ROUTE OF THE WHALERS

Routes
of the
Sailers
and
Whalers

VALPARAISO

MONTEVIDEO

CAPE HORN ROUTE N.Y. TO S.F.

A BARK FIGHTING
A CAPE HORN
STORM

CAPE
HORN

## PADDLE-WHEEL STEAMERS

**Big Day in the Bay**

It was the 28th of February, 1849. The guns at the mouth of San Francisco harbor boomed into the quiet morning.

Boom! Boom! Boom!

Excited people climbed to the top of Telegraph Hill. The black arms of a tower on the hill signaled that a vessel had been sighted.

A rider galloped over the sandy hills from his lookout by the beach.

"A steamer! A steamer! An honest-to-gosh paddle-wheel steamer is a-steamin' through the Gate," he panted.

It wasn't long before the steady "kachunk-kachunk" of paddle wheels was heard coming around Clark's Point.

44

And there she was! The *California!* The first American paddle-wheel steamer to enter San Francisco Bay.

The steamer dropped anchor. The cannons on five American warships anchored off Alcatraz Island fired a salute. Flags fluttered in the wind.

Commodore Thomas Ap Catesby Jones stood on the quarterdeck of his flagship, the *Ohio*.

"Man the yards!" he ordered.

Crews went aloft. The air was filled with lusty shouts. The *California's* passengers crowded to the rails and let out a mighty roar.

**Not Much Fun for Anyone**

Despite the excitement when she arrived in San Francisco, the *California's* first trip had not been much fun for anyone. She was barely out

of New York harbor when she had trouble with her engines. Then her commander, Captain Forbes, got sick. But the sturdy little steamer made a record run of twenty-six days to the port of Rio de Janeiro in Brazil. Here she filled her bunkers full of coal and her galley full of food. Then she started south.

The *California* was the first steamer to enter the strait discovered by Magellan in 1520. There were no good charts to show the narrow channel. The williwahs, or sudden squalls of wind and fog, buffeted the steamer night and day. Her log records six days for the passage, but many of these were spent at anchor waiting for fair wind and weather.

At Valparaiso, in Chile, a substitute for the sick captain had to come aboard. Mr. Forbes continued on the ship, but he was not in command.

On December 27, when the *California* reached Callao, Peru, she found eager miners waiting for a ship that could carry them to San Francisco. Seventeen cabin and eighty steerage passengers came aboard. For the first time, the officers and crew of the *California* heard the facts about the discovery of gold in California.

But what the ship found in Callao was nothing compared to what the *California* discovered in the little town of Panama City, Panama. Fifteen hundred would-be gold hunters had already crossed the Isthmus of Panama and were waiting for the steamer. A few of these held tickets on the *California,* bought before they left New York. As for all the rest, it was just bluff and swagger that got anyone aboard. The price of tickets went sky high. Three hundred dollars was thought a fair amount to pay for a chance to be the first into the gold fields.

Three hundred and sixty-five people crowded onto the little steamer, built to carry seventy-five. From the diary kept by Captain Forbes, we learn that the ship was "filled to cramnation with passengers and stores and everyone looking out for himself.... We have many on board of very high standing... but we also have many of the scum of creation, blackleg gamblers, thieves, runners, and drunkards, and if we make the trip without difficulty... I will be much surprised.... Handsome cushions and mattresses are brought on deck and laid on the wet and coal dust, and are spit upon and trodden on."

One clever miner hitched a hammock to the rigging and spent the passage there. Food was scarce, mostly old salt beef and bread with worms "an inch long," a passenger later reported. Off the coast of Mexico, the firemen mutinied in an argument over a stowaway discovered in the engine room. Putting into Mazatlán, in Mexico, the captain had the leaders of the mutiny arrested and hustled off to prison. Their places were filled by Mexicans.

Steaming north once more, the ship ran into fog. Then coal ran short. The fires died out. The sails were raised. The passengers were given axes and asked to make firewood out of doors, chairs, and tables. But not too much damage was done before 100 bags of coal were discovered hidden near the keel.

The fires were relighted. The fog lifted, and the *California* steamed into Monterey. Once more the passengers were asked to lend a hand. For five days, at $5 a day, every husky man aboard chopped wood onshore. At last enough fuel was stored below for the short run to San Francisco. No wonder passengers and crew alike let out a mighty roar as the *California* cast anchor off San Francisco. Only Captain Forbes and one loyal crew member were left on board by noon that day. Everybody else had already started for the gold fields.

**The Pacific Mail Steamship Company**

The *California* was the first of three paddle-wheel steamers built for the new Pacific Mail Steamship Company. These ships, the *California,* the *Oregon,* and the *Panama,* were built to carry the United States mail between Panama and Oregon.

The mail was first brought by steamer from New York to Chagres, on the eastern shore of the Isthmus of Panama. Then it was carried across the Isthmus to Panama City, where it was picked up for the trip to California. The steamers were to stop at San Diego, Santa Barbara, Monterey, and San Francisco.

Between 1849 and 1851, the Pacific Mail steamers had all they could do to carry passengers and mail between Panama and San Francisco. For this reason, they did not push north from San Francisco. Sailing ships carried the mail sacks and a few passengers on to Oregon.

Then, in 1851, a new steamer, the *Columbia,* was built in New York especially for the northwestern coastal trade. For several years, she was the only steamer on the route. Although the *Columbia* did not, at first, belong to the Pacific Mail, they soon bought her. She stopped at Humboldt Bay, Crescent City, Port Orford, and Coos Bay en route to the Columbia River and Puget Sound.

**Steamer Days**

Twice each month, the signal on the top of Telegraph Hill told the citizens of San Francisco that a steamer had been sighted. The people could tell what type of ship was entering the Bay by the way the signal arms were slanted.

When the signal arms showed that a Pacific Mail steamer was heading for Central Wharf, crowds gathered quickly—long lines waiting for mail, businessmen impatient for important news from the East, newspapermen eager for the latest happenings from all over the world, everyone waiting for letters from friends and families back home.

Thus, the first regular mail service between the East and West Coasts

of the United States was begun. What had been planned before the discovery of gold as a simple mail and passenger service for the sleepy West Coast towns, turned out to be a gold mine. The Pacific Mail Steamship Company was well on its way to fifty years of fame and fortune.

## Mail to China

In 1867, the thriving Pacific Mail Steamship Company was given a contract to carry the United States mail to Japan and China. The company's steamers, the *Colorado,* the *Great Republic,* the *China,* and several others, made the trip from San Francisco out to Hong Kong in 32 days and 10 hours. These side-wheelers were giant models of the *California,* built 20 years before. Their wooden hulls were 360 feet long. A single cylinder turned their huge paddle wheels, which were 40 feet across.

The return of one of these great ships from the Orient was as important an occasion as the arrival of one of the little steamers from Panama had been in the early days of San Francisco. Crowds collected. Boarding-house keepers fought with each other for customers. Cabdrivers pulled their horses up to the wharf to pick up first-class passengers as they hurried down the gangplank. Chinese swarmed up from the steerage with their bedding, clothes, and all that they owned slung over their shoulders on bamboo poles. American businessmen, missionaries, diplomats, naval officers, and tourists—these were the passengers who were willing to pay $300 apiece for a trip to and from Hong Kong.

## End of the Pacific Mail

The Pacific Mail side-wheelers were famous in their day, but these ships were the last of their kind. The British were already building iron ocean liners that were driven by propellers instead of by wooden paddle wheels. Soon other companies opened lines to the Orient. The Pacific Mail Steamship Company built more up-to-date ships and kept them running until 1925. Then the Dollar Line, or the American President Lines as we know it today, took over the old Pacific Mail.

# RIVER STEAMERS

### Off for Hangtown

"Take a boat! Take a boat! Take *my* boat! Right this way, gentlemen, for the fastest, safest boat to the gold fields." This was the cry the gold-seekers heard as they stepped ashore in San Francisco.

If the gold hunters took a boat up the Sacramento River to Sacramento, they could walk to Hangtown. Hangtown was close to the spot on the American River where James Marshall first found gold.

If the would-be miners took a boat up the San Joaquin River and landed at Stockton, they were close to the southern mines. They could easily reach Bedbug, Chucklehead Diggings, or Skunk Gulch.

When the Gold Rush started, there were only a few flat-bottom scow sloops, scow schooners, and rowboats to take the miners up the rivers. But the gold hunters wanted to get to the mines as fast as they could. The miners needed bigger and faster boats. What the miners needed were ships that ran by steam.

**The Senator Arrives**

Just five months after the *California* left New York on her first trip to San Francisco, another side-wheeler, the *Senator,* paddled her way through the Strait of Magellan. At Panama City, hundreds of gold hunters wanted to board the *Senator.* Her captain was glad to oblige at $500 a ticket, and two hundred miners jammed aboard.

Seven months and seventeen days after she left New York, the *Senator* arrived in San Francisco. The crew barely had time to clean out her boilers before she was put to work on the Sacramento River. Everyone wanted to ride on her, and no wonder! It took the sloops and schooners three to four days to run from San Francisco up to Sacramento. The *Senator* made it in nine hours.

51

### The Beautiful New Steamer Chrysopolis

On the second of June, 1860, a full moon rose over San Francisco Bay. The bright moon shone on the water and the land and on the shipyard of John North. It shone on the faces of the five thousand people eagerly awaiting the launching of a brand new steamer, the *Chrysopolis*.

Out in the Bay, the river boat *Eclipse* stood by, lights gayly blinking from every porthole. The tugboat *Columbia* kept up steam, just in case she might be needed.

The *Chrysopolis,* which means "golden city," was named for San Francisco, for in those days San Francisco was certainly the city of gold. John North had designed and built the steamship. The Neptune Iron Works of New York had built her engine. The clipper ship, *Asa Eldridge,* sailed the engine around the Horn for the California Steam Navigation Company. The California Steam Navigation Company was, for many years, the most important steamship company in California. It owned most of the steamboats that ran on the inland rivers.

The crowd cheered. The *Eclipse* and the *Columbia* blew their whistles. The largest and most beautiful steamboat ever built in the West slid down the ways. She was as fine, if not finer, than the fancy paddle-wheel steamers running on the Hudson River, and certainly as good as any to be found on the Mississippi.

Two months later, the *Chrysopolis* was ready for work on the Sacramento River. She proved to be as fast as she was beautiful. "One feels a sensation like riding on air when steaming up the river on the *Chrysopolis,*" wrote an early passenger.

There was space enough for one thousand people on deck. Her cabins had beds enough to sleep 100. There was beautiful wood in her saloon. Her tables were covered with marble. Huge mirrors hung on her walls, as well as four beautiful paintings of early California days.

The run from San Francisco up the Sacramento River was not an easy one. It was 117 miles of crooked, winding water. But it was the most important inland waterway in all of California. Up this river went the gold-seekers on their way to the mines. Down this river they came again, some rich, some poor. Politicians rode the river boats on their

STERN-
WHEELER

way to the state capital at Sacramento. Farmers came and went from the rich Sacramento Valley. Merchants and businessmen, setting up stores and bringing up machinery for the mines, all traveled the Sacramento. The United States mail was carried on the river steamers until the railroads took over the job.

The *Chrysopolis* left San Francisco three times a week at four o'clock in the afternoon. She would spend the night in Sacramento and head back at two o'clock the following afternoon. Her record run from Sacramento back to San Francisco was five hours and nineteen minutes.

## A River Race

The California Steam Navigation Company was not the only company running boats to Sacramento. The arrival of a new steamer belonging to another company was usually the occasion for an exciting river race. One of the first and most famous of these races was that between the *Chrysopolis* and the fast new steamer *Nevada*.

Both boats were loading at a wharf in Sacramento, perhaps even side by side. The news spread. There would surely be a race that day!

Captain Phillips of the *Nevada* kept a careful eye on Captain Chadwick of the *Chrysopolis*. Suddenly the *Nevada's* whistle blew. "Cast off," a deckhand shouted. The *Nevada* pulled out into the river. The *Chrysopolis* took nine minutes to get her paddles turning.

The race was on. Both captains carried orders reading: "Win, no matter what!" This meant shovel on coal, coal, and more coal! Build up the steam! Never mind if many a steamboat had been blown sky high by a bursting boiler! Captain Chadwick and Captain Phillips were willing to take the chance.

News of the race spread down the river. Bets were quickly made. Indians, farmers, and storekeepers came down to watch. Everyone cheered as the "flaming devils" passed.

A Sacramento paper reported the finish: "The *Nevada* came sneezing and blazing...her flaming chimneys lit up the atmosphere. The sight... was truly gorgeous." But the *Chrysopolis* had already glided smoothly up to her dock—the winner by ten minutes!

53

SIDE-WHEELER

### The Man Who Stole a Steamer

Captain Ned Wakeman was not a man to take "no" for an answer. The undersheriff of New York City told him that the paddle-wheel steamer *New World* was not to leave New York harbor until all the money owed for her building was paid. But Captain Wakeman had other ideas. How could a ship make money to pay her debts lying at anchor? He knew there was money enough to be made on the rivers of California. That was where the *New World* belonged.

The undersheriff and several of his marshals came to live aboard the river boat just to make sure, the sheriff explained, that nobody "gets any fancy ideas." Captain Wakeman filled the bunkers with coal. "Just to run her around the harbor," he explained to the sheriff. Then Captain Wakeman hired a crew and hid them below. He loaded all the food he could stow away during the night while the sheriff and his men were sleeping in their elegant cabins above.

The first the sheriff knew of all this was when he awoke to find himself halfway out of New York harbor. When he tried to place Captain Wakeman under arrest, the sheriff was faced with a grim Ned Wakeman and an even grimmer-looking revolver.

"Sheriff," the captain explained, "on land, you are the law. At sea, only the captain gives orders, and I order you and your men ashore."

54

The unhappy sheriff and his marshals soon stood deep in a New Jersey mud flat. There was nothing left to do but shake their fists at the fast-disappearing *New World*. Captain Wakeman had stolen a ship and was sailing without any papers, for his were locked in the sheriff's New York office. In the eyes of the law, Ned Wakeman was a pirate!

Soon after leaving New York, the steamer ran into a storm. She was almost battered to kindling wood. River boats were built light and shallow for steaming about inland waters, not for battling high waves and strong winds. Captain Wakeman ordered a false bow to be built to protect the forward deck and windows. The walking beam gave way and almost crashed through the deck. But somehow the *New World* came through this storm, and several others as well. Captain Wakeman knew he must put into port for repairs before heading toward the Strait of Magellan. But how could he do this without any papers?

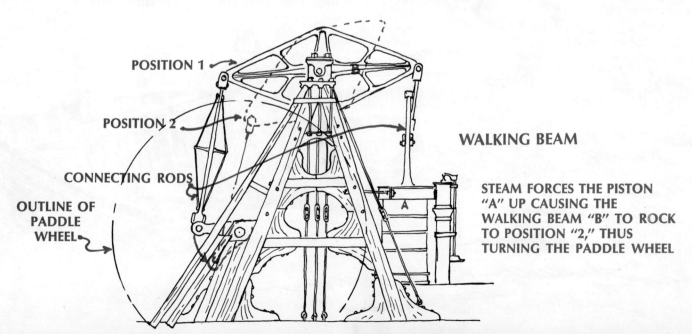

POSITION 1

POSITION 2

CONNECTING RODS

OUTLINE OF PADDLE WHEEL

WALKING BEAM

STEAM FORCES THE PISTON "A" UP CAUSING THE WALKING BEAM "B" TO ROCK TO POSITION "2," THUS TURNING THE PADDLE WHEEL

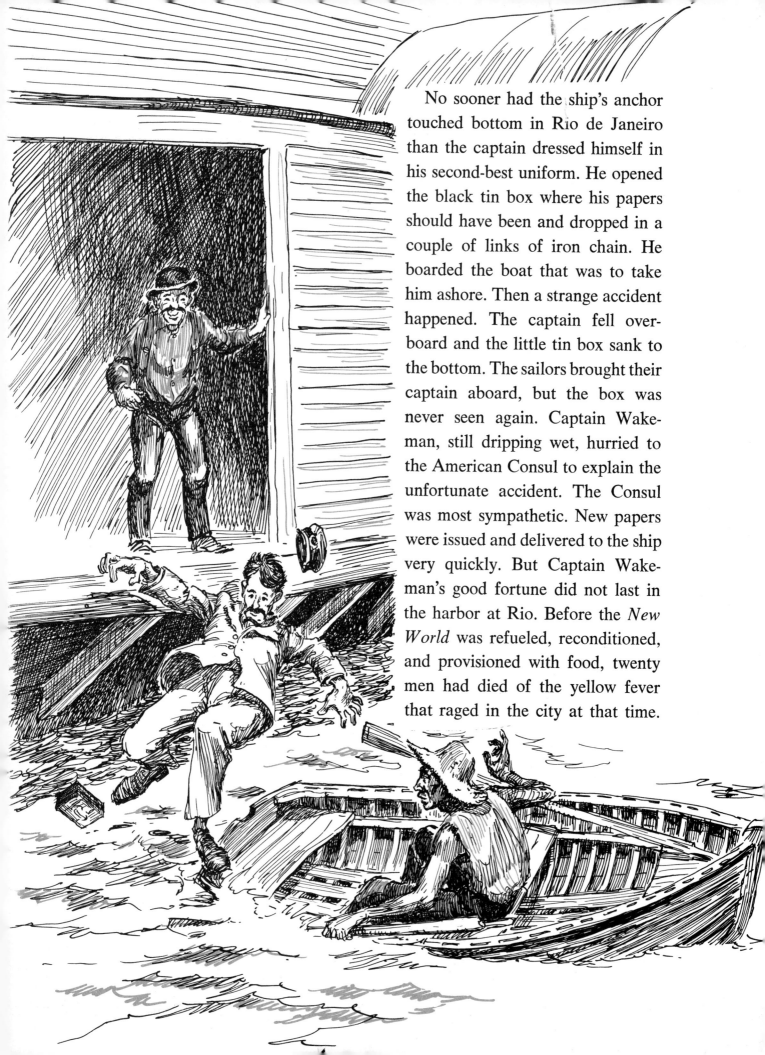

No sooner had the ship's anchor touched bottom in Rio de Janeiro than the captain dressed himself in his second-best uniform. He opened the black tin box where his papers should have been and dropped in a couple of links of iron chain. He boarded the boat that was to take him ashore. Then a strange accident happened. The captain fell overboard and the little tin box sank to the bottom. The sailors brought their captain aboard, but the box was never seen again. Captain Wakeman, still dripping wet, hurried to the American Consul to explain the unfortunate accident. The Consul was most sympathetic. New papers were issued and delivered to the ship very quickly. But Captain Wakeman's good fortune did not last in the harbor at Rio. Before the *New World* was refueled, reconditioned, and provisioned with food, twenty men had died of the yellow fever that raged in the city at that time.

Despite this loss, the *New World* pushed on. She made her way through the Strait of Magellan in three days and headed north, up the coast of South America. At Callao, in Peru, Captain Wakeman was told that the news of his escape from New York with the steamer had already reached Panama City by way of the Isthmus of Panama. Not only had the news reached the city, but it was said that two United States marshals were awaiting the captain's arrival.

But this didn't disturb Captain Wakeman. Indeed, he felt sure there would be business for his steamer if only he could reach Panama in time to outwit the waiting marshals. Hurrying north, he brought his ship into the harbor of Panama City at night and anchored behind a small island. Then, disguising himself as a miner in boots, old pants, and red shirt, he went ashore. It was just as he had thought. The town was bursting with gold-seekers eager to get to San Francisco.

The next morning the *New World* steamed into the harbor. Captain Wakeman stood in the pilothouse. A mob of screaming, pushing miners crowded the beaches. Two United States marshals also waited ashore. When the crowd learned what the men of the law were waiting for, they threatened a little rough treatment if the marshals stopped the *New World* from sailing. But there was no need for bloodshed. The terrified marshals made themselves scarce just as fast as their shaking legs would carry them. The *New World* sailed for San Francisco three days later with 217 miners aboard and $65,100 stored in the captain's cabin.

On arrival in San Francisco, four months after leaving New York, the *New World's* owner William Brown paid off all that he owed for the steamer and had a tidy sum for the bank besides. The *New World* was desperately needed in California and quickly started her run on the Sacramento River. Ned Wakeman had been right. The steamer was to make more money on the river than even *he* had dreamed possible.

### The End of the Floating Palaces

In 1869, the railroad ran East to West. Tracks were laid all the way from New York to Sacramento, then down to Oakland and to Vallejo by the Bay. Ferryboats picked up the passengers and freight at Oakland or Vallejo and carried them across the Bay to San Francisco. The days of the floating palaces were almost over.

After the coming of the railroad, big stern-wheel steamers like the *Delta King* and the *Delta Queen* were built and did useful service for awhile, but finally trains, trucks, and automobiles took their work away. The Sacramento River was no longer the busiest roadway in the West.

The *Chrysopolis* was remade into a ferryboat in 1875. Her name was changed to the *Oakland,* and she paddled back and forth across the Bay for over sixty years. Then the two great bridges, the Golden Gate Bridge and the San Francisco-Oakland Bay Bridge, were finished and even the need for ferryboats was over.

Smaller stern-wheel boats were built to carry freight and a few passengers on the rivers, sloughs, and bays that branched out from San Francisco Bay. But the captain of the *Petaluma,* a small river boat made this entry in his log on August 24, 1950: "After 35 years, 8 months, and 9 days, we tie up for good. This ends 103 years of stern-wheel river navigation on San Francisco Bay and tributaries."

*The ferryboat* Eureka *saw many years of service in San Francisco Bay. Built in 1890, the* Eureka *at one time claimed to be the fastest double-ended ferryboat in all the world. She could handle 2,300 passengers and 120 automobiles at once. This fine old boat has been restored by the Maritime Museum and the State Division of Beaches and Parks and is on view at the Hyde Street Pier in San Francisco.*

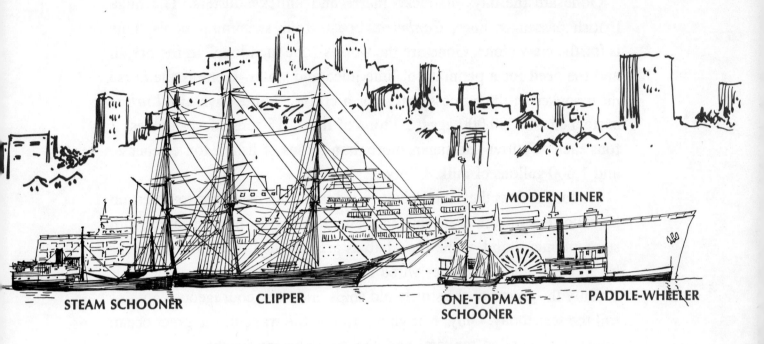

STEAM SCHOONER   CLIPPER   ONE-TOPMAST SCHOONER   MODERN LINER   PADDLE-WHEELER

# YESTERDAY AND TODAY

What has become of the deep-sea sailers, the whalers, the paddle-wheel steamers, the ships that opened the West? Where are the ships that sailed the world, heavy with whale oil, grain, and Douglas fir? Great steel ships, run by huge engines, have taken the place of the ships that sailed by wind alone. Propellers have replaced the paddle wheels.

Freighters, oil tankers, beautiful passenger liners—these are the new ships built to carry tons of cargo and thousands of people around the world. A single freighter today can swing 400 automobiles aboard and still have space left over.

The clipper *Stag Hound* was a ship of 1,535 tons and was 215 feet long. The modern *S. S. Lurline,* the largest passenger liner of the Matson Navigation Company, is a ship of 26,150 tons and is 638 feet long, which is almost twice as long as the average football field.

The side-wheelers of the Pacific Mail Steamship Company took thirty-two days and ten hours to go from San Francisco to Hong Kong. Today, the *President Cleveland* and the *President Wilson,* two sister ships of the American President Lines, cruise from San Francisco to Hong Kong in eighteen days.

59

Gone are the days of bucko mates and knuckle-dusters. The huge British passenger liner, *Canberra*, boasts four swimming pools. One is for the crew alone. Gone are the worms "one inch long" in the bread, and the need for a pannikin of lime juice and water. Gone is the horse meat soaked in the harness cask. For a cruise of nine days, the *Lurline* is stocked with 30,000 eggs, 20 tons of meat, 15 tons of vegetables, 2 tons each of butter and sugar, more than 3 tons of fish, 1 ton of cheese, and 1,600 gallons of milk.

No longer does the captain have a piano swung on board to entertain his wife. Passengers are treated to Cinemascope in huge theaters with stereophonic sound, while their babies are watched in luxurious cabins by an electronic baby sitter wired to a central switchboard.

Only the ghosts of the sturdy old ships and their courageous captains sail the seas today. Only their ghosts follow the wake of the great ocean liners, the oil-filled tankers, and the cargo-heavy freighters, for these are the ships that have taken the place of the sailers, the whalers, and the paddle-wheel steamers—the ships that opened the West.

# BIBLIOGRAPHY

Bone, David W. THE BRASSBOUNDER. New York: E. P. Dutton & Co., 1921.

Chapelle, Howard I. THE HISTORY OF AMERICAN SAILING SHIPS. New York: W. W. Norton & Co., 1935.

Clark, Arthur H. THE CLIPPER SHIP ERA. New York: G. P. Putnam's Sons, 1910.

Cutler, Carl C. GREYHOUNDS OF THE SEA: Story of the American Clipper Ship. New York: Halcyon House, 1930.

Dana, Richard Henry. TWO YEARS BEFORE THE MAST. New York: Modern Library, Random House, 1936.

Davis, Charles G. SHIP MODEL BUILDER'S ASSISTANT. Salem, Mass.: Marine Research Society, 1926. (Reprinted New York, N. Y.: Sweetman Publishing Co.) A book of fascinating information about everything to do with ships.

——. THE WAYS OF THE SEA. New York: The Rudder Publishing Co., 1930. Equipment of a sailing ship and how it is used.

Dillon, Richard H. EMBARCADERO. New York: Coward McCann, 1957.

Downey, Joseph T. THE CRUISE OF THE PORTSMOUTH: A Sailor's View of the Naval Conquest of California, 1845-1847. New Haven and London: Yale University Press, 1958.

Hare, Lloyd C. M. SALTED TORIES. Mystic, Connecticut: Marine Historical Association, 1960. Good account of whaling out of San Francisco.

Harlan, George H., and Fisher, Clement, Jr. OF WALKING BEAMS AND PADDLE WHEELS. Oakland: Bay Books, Ltd., 1951.

Harlow, F. P. CHANTYING ABOARD AMERICAN SHIPS. Barre, Mass.: Barre Publishing Company, 1962.

——. THE MAKING OF A SAILOR, or SEA LIFE ABOARD A YANKEE SQUARE-RIGGER. Salem, Mass.: Marine Research Society, 1928.

Hohman, E. R. THE AMERICAN WHALEMAN. New York: Longmans Green & Co., 1928.

Huycke, H. D. "The Great Star Fleet," YACHTING MAGAZINE, February and March, 1960. (Reprinted San Francisco Maritime Museum, 1960.)

Kemble, John H. SAN FRANCISCO BAY, A PICTORIAL MARITIME HISTORY. Cambridge: Cornell Maritime Press, 1957.

——. "Side-Wheelers Across Pacific," AMERICAN NEPTUNE, II, 1:5-38, Jan., 1942.

Kittredge, Henry C. SHIPMASTERS OF CAPE COD. Boston: Houghton Mifflin Co., 1935.

Krythe, Maymie. PORT ADMIRAL: PHINEAS BANNING. San Francisco: California Historical Society, 1957.

Lewis, Oscar. SEA ROUTES TO THE GOLD FIELDS. New York: A. Knopf, 1945.

Lubbock, Alfred Basil. THE DOWN-EASTERS. Boston: Charles E. Lauriat Co., 1929.

——. THE LAST OF THE WINDJAMMERS. Boston: Charles E. Lauriat Co., 1927.

McArthur, Walter. LAST DAYS OF SAIL ON THE WEST COAST. San Francisco: San Francisco Press of the J. K. Barry Co., 1929.

McKay, Richard C. SOME FAMOUS SAILING SHIPS AND THEIR BUILDER, DONALD McKAY. New York: G. P. Putnam's Sons, 1928.

MacMullen, Jerry. PADDLE-WHEEL DAYS IN CALIFORNIA. Stanford: Stanford University Press, 1944.

McNairn, Jack, and MacMullen, Jerry. SHIPS OF THE REDWOOD COAST. Stanford: Stanford University Press, 1945.

Matthews, Frederick C. AMERICAN MERCHANT SHIPS. Salem, Mass.: Marine Research Society, 1930. History of Down-Easters, 2 vols.

Mills, Randall V. STERN-WHEELERS UP THE COLUMBIA. Palo Alto: Pacific Books, 1947.

Newell, Gordon, and Williamson, Joe. PACIFIC STEAMBOATS. Seattle: Superior Publishing Co., 1958.

——. PADDLEWHEEL PIRATE. New York: E. P. Dutton & Co., 1959.

Reisenberg, Felix, Jr. GOLDEN GATE. New York and London: Alfred A. Knopf, 1940.

——. UNDER SAIL. London: Jonathan Capt, Ltd., 1925.

Trott, Harlan, SCHOONER THAT CAME HOME: FINAL VOYAGE OF THE C. A. THAYER. Cambridge: Cornell Maritime Press, 1958.

# GLOSSARY

**Afterdeck**—The part of a deck toward the stern (back) of a ship.

**Belaying Pin**—A wooden or iron pin on a vessel's rail to which sailors tied ropes.

**Belaying Pin Soup**—Beating a crewman with a belaying pin.

**Blood Money**—Money paid by a captain to a crimp for the delivery of a sailor.

**Breakwater**—A wall for breaking the force of waves in a harbor.

**Bucko Mate**—A tough officer who often used force to control sailors.

**Bunkers**—Large bins or storage places for fuel on a steamship.

**Cabin Passenger**—A ship's passenger traveling first class rather than steerage.

**Crimp**—One who shanghais.

**Dogwatch**—One of two watches of two hours each on ship—from 4 p.m. to 6 p.m. or from 6 p.m. to 8 p.m.

**Furl**—To wrap sails tightly when not in use.

**Galley**—The kitchen aboard ship.

**Hold**—The inside of a vessel below the lower deck where cargo is stored.

**Hull**—The body of a ship.

**Keel**—The backbone of a ship.

**Lee Bow**—The side of the ship at the bow, away from the wind.

**Log**—The book in which record of a voyage is kept by the captain or mate.

**Man the Yards**—The naval order for sailors to climb up and stand in a row on the yards on special occasions.

**Mate**—An officer who ranks below the captain.

**Merchantman**—A trading or cargo vessel.

**Nantucket Sleigh Ride**—A ride in a whaleboat when pulled through the water by a whale.

**Planking**—The heavy boards forming the hull and decks of a vessel.

**Port**—An opening in a ship's side through which air, light, and cargo may pass, or through which cannons may be fired.

**Quarterdeck**—The part of the poop-deck kept just for the captain and officers.

**Ribs**—The frame of a vessel, running from keel to deck.

**Rigging**—The ropes, wires, and chains that are used to support the masts and trim (control) the sails of a ship.

**Sailers**—Vessels that are moved by the wind rather than by engines.

**Sailors**—Men who work on ships.

**Saloon**—A ship's dining-sitting room for the captain, the officers, and the passengers.

**Shanghai**—To kidnap a man and put him on an outbound vessel, collecting his future pay from the captain.

**Steerage**—The cheapest quarters for passengers, usually below decks.

**Tiffin**—Luncheon, or tea.

**Vessel**—Any type of water craft.

**Watch**—A period of time on duty, usually 4 hours long, changing at 12 o'clock, 4 o'clock, and 8 o'clock. 1. To be on duty. 2. The half, or today, the third of the crew and officers who are on duty.

**Ways**—The slightly slanting frame on which a vessel is built and on which it slides into the water when launched.

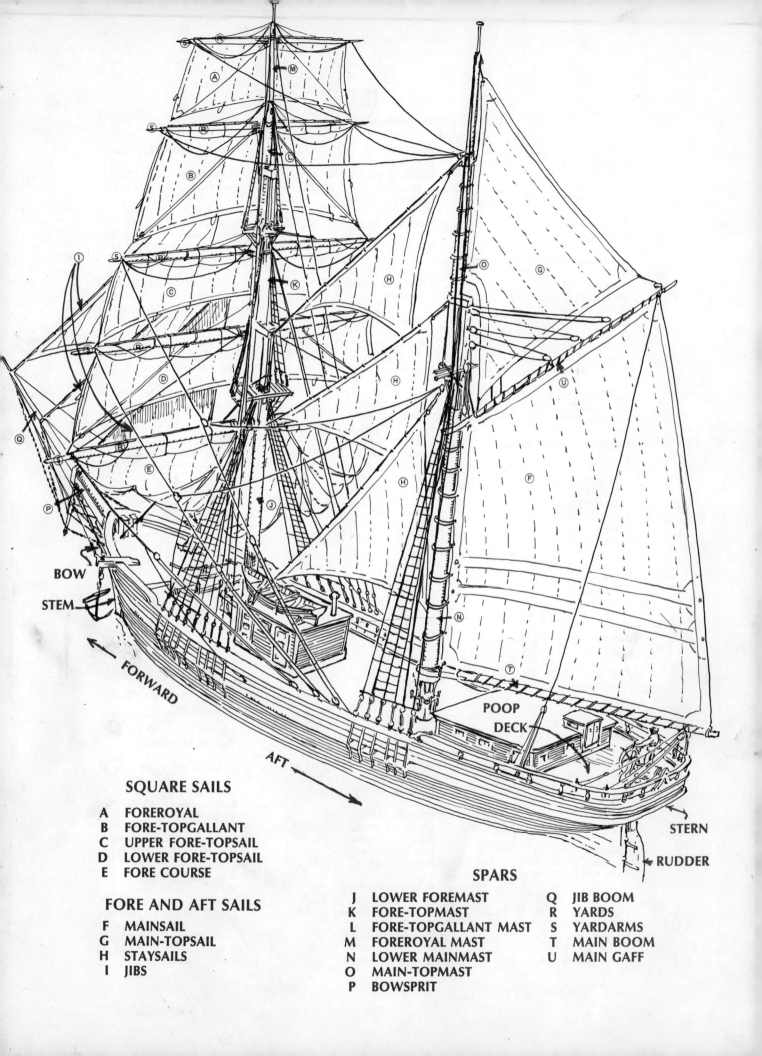

BOW

STEM

FORWARD

AFT

POOP

DECK

STERN

RUDDER

## SQUARE SAILS

A FOREROYAL
B FORE-TOPGALLANT
C UPPER FORE-TOPSAIL
D LOWER FORE-TOPSAIL
E FORE COURSE

## FORE AND AFT SAILS

F MAINSAIL
G MAIN-TOPSAIL
H STAYSAILS
I JIBS

## SPARS

J LOWER FOREMAST
K FORE-TOPMAST
L FORE-TOPGALLANT MAST
M FOREROYAL MAST
N LOWER MAINMAST
O MAIN-TOPMAST
P BOWSPRIT

Q JIB BOOM
R YARDS
S YARDARMS
T MAIN BOOM
U MAIN GAFF

# INDEX

Heavy numbers (**42**) refer to pages on which maps appear